HOCKEY SUPERSTARS
Past, Present, and Future

Jennifer Rivkin

CRABTREE
Publishing Company
www.crabtreebooks.com

Author: Jennifer Rivkin

Publishing plan research and development:
Reagan Miller, Crabtree Publishing Company

Editors: Marcia Abramson, Kelly Spence

Proofreader: Wendy Scavuzzo

Photo research: Melissa McClellan

Cover Design: Samara Parent

Design: T. J. Choleva

Prepress technician: Samara Parent

Print and production coordinator: Katherine Berti

Consultant: Jeff Reynolds, Technical Director of hockey for Chedoke Minor hockey

Developed and produced for Crabtree Publishing by BlueAppleWorks Inc.

Images on cover (top left, clockwise): Alexander Ovechkin, Washington Capitals; Mario Lemieux, Pittsburgh Penguins; Marie-Philip Poulin, Canadian National Team

Image on title page: Blackhawks Captain Jonathan Toews battles Penguins Captain Sidney Crosby

Photographs:
Front Cover: AP Images: AP*MAC* (top right)
Keystone Press: © Ben Pelosse (bottom left)
Thinkstock: Rob Carr (top left)

Interior: Corbis: © Mike Blake/Reuters/Corbis (p 8); © Bettmann/Corbis (p 18 left, 26)
Shutterstock.com: © Jai Agnish (TOC, p 18–19 top); © B Calkins (page toppers); © Shooter Bob Square Lenses (hand & puck); © Matthew Jacques (p 5 right, 10–11 bottom); © Iurii Osadchi (p 9 bottom, 13 top, 17); © Scott Prokop (p 10–11 top, p 22–23); © photosthatrock (p 11, 27 top); © Sven Hoppe (p 18–19 bottom); © Photo Works (p 25 left); © Tumar (p 28–29 top); © Rob Marmion (p 28 –29 bottom); © Lorraine Swanson (p 30)
Public Domain: Conrad Poirier (p 7 top right); William James Topley/Bibliothèque et Archives Canada/PA-043029 (p 7 bottom); Gazette/Library and Archives Canada/PA-108357 (p 9 top); Library and Archives Canada/PA-195211(p 25 right)
Keystone Press: © Mike Wulf (title page, 16, 20); © Gerry Angus (p 4); © Detroit Free Press (p 6); © Billy Hurst (p 14); © Victor Junco (p 15); © Anthony Nesmith (p 19 right); © Mike Strasinger (p 21); © Duncan Williams (p 23 right); © Andy Blenkush (p 28 left); © Patrick T Fallon (p 29 bottom right)
Zumapress.com: © Keith Charles (p 10 left); © Michael Kappeler (p 13 bottom); © Bob Fina (p 27 bottom); © Andy Martin Jr. (p 29 top)
Creative Commons: Resolute (p 5 left); Jvuollo (p 6 top left); Håkan Dahlström (p 12); Rick Dikeman (p 22 right); Kristina Servant (p 24)

Library and Archives Canada Cataloguing in Publication

Rivkin, Jennifer, author
        Hockey superstars : past, present, and future / Jennifer Rivkin.

(Hockey source)
Includes index.
Issued in print and electronic formats.
ISBN 978-0-7787-0766-0 (bound).--ISBN 978-0-7787-0715-8 (pbk.).--
ISBN 978-1-4271-7682-0 (pdf).--ISBN 978-1-4271-7678-3 (html)

        1. Hockey players--Biography--Juvenile literature. I. Title.

GV848.5.A1R58 2014   j796.962092'2   C2014-903830-5
                                                                        C2014-903831-3

Library of Congress Cataloging-in-Publication Data

CIP available at the Library of Congress

Crabtree Publishing Company

www.crabtreebooks.com   1-800-387-7650

Printed in the U.S.A./092014/JA20140811

Published in Canada
Crabtree Publishing
616 Welland Ave.
St. Catharines, ON
L2M 5V6

Published in the United States
Crabtree Publishing
PMB 59051
350 Fifth Avenue, 59th Floor
New York, New York 10118

Published in the United Kingdom
Crabtree Publishing
Maritime House
Basin Road North, Hove
BN41 1WR

Published in Australia
Crabtree Publishing
3 Charles Street
Coburg North
VIC 3058

TABLE OF CONTENTS

LET'S PLAY HOCKEY!

THE RISE TO THE TOP

The talented hockey players that become professionals in the National Hockey League (NHL) are the top athletes in their sport. They tear across the ice effortlessly, making incredible **dekes**, passes, and shots on goal. Even among the pros, there are those who stand above the rest. These hockey legends will be remembered forever on **memorabilia**, in books, movies and—most importantly—in the hearts of hockey fans!

Superstars practice for thousands of hours to be the best players on the ice!

Everyone Counts

To create a winning team, **scouts**, coaches, and managers look for strong players to fill every position on the ice. Many superstars have to work their way up through the levels

The Toronto Marlies and Hamilton Bulldogs are the affiliated AHL teams for the Toronto Maple Leafs and Montreal Canadiens.

of **amateur** hockey before going pro. Half of all NHL players develop their skills in the junior Canadian Hockey League (CHL). The American Hockey League (AHL) is a professional league that is a stepping stone to playing in the NHL. Every NHL team is **affiliated**, or connected, with a team in the (AHL).

Never Give Up

Martin St. Louis has stuck it out through difficult games and a tough path to the NHL. At just 5'8" (173 cm), he was small for pro hockey. He made up for his size with his amazing speed and **hockey sense**, or natural feel for the game. Still, he was passed over by every team in the league during the NHL **draft** the year he graduated from college. Rather than admitting defeat, St. Louis kept playing and was eventually signed by the Calgary Flames. In 2000, he joined the Tampa Bay Lightning. He was the NHL's high scorer and Most Valuable Player (MVP) in 2004, and led the Lightning to their first ever Stanley Cup victory.

St. Louis was traded to the New York Rangers in 2014 and helped them get to the Stanley Cup final.

HOCKEY'S FIRST SUPERSTARS

Hockey games were not televised widely until the 1950s—years after Gordie Howe and Maurice "The Rocket" Richard joined the NHL. But even though most hockey fans had not seen these two superstars with their own eyes, making magic on ice, they had heard about the hockey legends.

Mr. Hockey

Gordie Howe joined the Detroit Red Wings in 1946 when he was just 18 years old. At 6' tall and over 200 pounds (183 cm and 91 kg), he used his size to his advantage. Early in his career, he was known as being a fighter. Later, it was his spectacular hockey skills and energy that people noticed—he could play any position and was always ready for another shift. The right winger went on to become one of the top five scorers in the NHL for 20 straight seasons.

*Howe was **ambidextrous**, which means that he could shoot left or right.*

The Rocket

Maurice Richard joined the Montreal Canadiens in 1942 and started out with a bang. He scored·five goals in the first 16 games. He led his team to a Stanley Cup victory the next year in 1943. He became the league's first player to score 50 goals in a single season. Richard, who was called "The Rocket" because of his speed, was also known for being tough. He was once knocked unconscious during a game and still managed to score the winning goal after he woke up. He also played well under pressure, scoring 82 playoff goals—six of them in overtime.

In 1999, the NHL named a trophy after The Rocket for the league's top goal scorer.

Girl Power

The first documented women's ice hockey game took place in the late 1800s. However, it wasn't until almost 100 years later that women's hockey really took off. The first International Ice Hockey Federation (IIHF) World Women's Championship was held in 1990. Then, in 1998, women's hockey became an Olympic sport. Female players still don't have a paid professional team, but today's stars are working hard to change that. Since more girls are playing now than ever before, a paid pro team may be just around the corner.

When men headed for Europe during World War I, women got their first chance to play real hockey. Eva Ault became a fan favorite playing for the Ottawa Alerts, earning the nickname "Queen of the Ice." Once the war ended, so did the careers of the first female players.

HISTORY'S GREATEST TEAMS

Like the individual superstars who have made their mark on the game, there are larger-than-life teams that will go down in history. Each had a finely tuned collection of players working together as a single unit.

Edmonton Oilers: 1983–1990

In the 1980s, if a person was talking about pro hockey, it was almost a guarantee that the Edmonton Oilers' name would come up. The NHL team won the Stanley Cup five times in six years, starting in the 1983–84 season. For many of those years, the team was led by hockey legend Wayne Gretzky, who played nine seasons with the Oilers. He was voted the league MVP for eight of nine seasons. But Gretzky didn't win those Cups alone. The team had great coaching, a strong **offense**, or attacking line, and a skilled **defense**, or defending skills.

The Edmonton Oilers celebrate a Stanley Cup win.

Montreal Canadiens: 1956–1960, 1964–1969, 1975–1979

The Montreal Canadiens (nicknamed "the Habs") are truly part of hockey history. The team was founded in 1909, before the NHL ever existed. Since they joined the league, the Canadiens have won an astounding 24 Stanley Cups. That's more than any other team in the NHL. In fact, the next closest team—the Toronto Maple Leafs—have only 13. The Canadiens have dominated through teamwork, perseverance, and the help of superstars, including Maurice "The Rocket" Richard and Guy Lafleur.

The Montreal Canadiens in 1942. The "C" and "H" on their jerseys stands for "Club de Hockey Canadien," the team's name in French.

USA vs. Canada: Women's National Teams

If there is an international competition, such as the Olympics or World Championships, it is almost certain that the American and Canadian women's hockey teams will meet in the finals. These two teams have always commanded the world of women's hockey and the rivalry between them is fierce. They have played against each other in all 15 IIHF World Championship finals.

The tension between the American and Canadian women's teams make their games exciting to watch!

He shoots, he scores! The best forwards in hockey skate hard toward the **opposition**'s goal, weaving around players who get in their way, to take stunning shots on goal or pass to a teammate who is in a better scoring position. Many superstars can play any of the forward positions: right wing, left wing, and center.

Steven Stamkos

For 2008's number-one draft pick, hard work is the name of the game. Growing up, Steven Stamkos worked hard to perfect his shot. He practiced shooting 300–400 pucks a day. Later, his workouts included sprinting while dragging a sled loaded with up to 150 pounds (68 kg) of weight. Stamkos even swapped junk food for healthy, organic food. It all paid off. The center for the Tampa Bay Lightning was the NHL's leading goal scorer in 2010 and 2012.

STATS

Born: 02/07/90
Markham, ON, Canada

Position: Center
Shoots right
Team: #91 Tampa Bay Lightning, Captain

Sidney Crosby

Today, many hockey players dream of being a top goal scorer like "Sid the Kid." In 2005, at just 18, the Pittsburgh Penguins selected him first in the draft. That year, some people called the draft the "Sidney Crosby Sweepstakes." Adding Crosby to a team was like winning the lottery! Crosby didn't disappoint. The center was named the league's **Rookie** of the Year after his first season. At 20, he became the youngest player to ever captain an NHL team and was also the league's top scorer and MVP. Two years later, he led the Penguins to a Stanley Cup victory.

STATS

Born: 08/07/87
Cole Harbour, NS, Canada

Position: Center
Shoots left

Team: #87 Pittsburgh Penguins, Captain

Cool Fact!

Many hockey players are superstitious and have pre-game rituals or routines. Before a game, Sidney Crosby eats the same meal—a peanut butter and jelly sandwich! He also refuses to let anyone touch his sticks after he tapes them before a game. If anyone does, he has to retape them.

SIDNEY CROSBY

Wayne Gretzky

Wayne Gretzky is one of the most talented players the game has ever seen. There's a good reason he is called "The Great One." He learned to skate, stickhandle, and shoot on his family's backyard rink in Brantford, Ontario. There, he developed the speed and skill to outplay and outskate players that were much older than him. After he signed with the Edmonton Oilers in 1979, Gretzky began shattering record after record. From 1981, he won seven straight scoring titles. Gretzky was also an amazing passer, with 1,963 assists in his career. Most hockey fans were devastated when Gretzky was traded to the Los Angeles Kings in 1988. He finished his career playing with the New York Rangers.

WAYNE GRETZKY

Gretzky smashed the record for most goals in one season with a new record of 92—16 more than the previous record holder!

"A good hockey player plays where the puck is. A great hockey player plays where the puck is going to be."
— *Wayne Gretzky*

Cool Fact!

Wayne Gretzky always tucked in the right side of his hockey jersey. Many players copied him. Now, the NHL plans to enforce a rule that forbids players from tucking.

Hayley Wickenheiser

This powerhouse player leaves fans awestruck as one of the most dominating forces in women's hockey. Wickenheiser was only 15 when she began playing for the Canadian Women's National Team. She has continued to improve throughout her career, winning an Olympic medal every year since women's hockey was included in the Games: silver in 1998 and gold in 2002, 2006, 2010, and 2014. In 2003, Wickenheiser made international history as the first female player to score in a men's professional game while playing in Finland.

Wickenheiser was given the honor of holding the Canadian flag at the opening ceremonies of the 2014 Olympics in Sochi, Russia.

HAYLEY WICKENHEISER

Wickenheiser was named one of Sports Illustrated's *"Top 20 Toughest Athletes in the World" in 2008.*

STATS

Born: 08/12/78
Shaunavon, SK, Canada

Position: Forward
Shoots right

Team: Canadian National Team

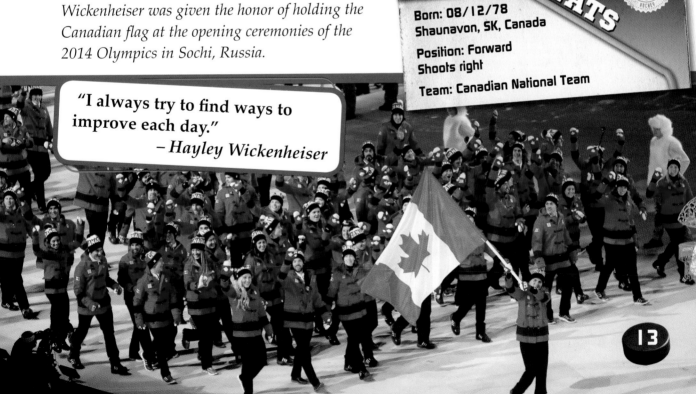

"I always try to find ways to improve each day."
 – *Hayley Wickenheiser*

Alexander Ovechkin

This right winger was playing pro hockey in Russia by the time he was 16. But Ovechkin always imagined playing in the NHL. When he was 17, the Washington Capitals signed him as the number-one draft pick. It wasn't long before he proved his worth—Ovechkin scored two goals in the first four minutes of his first game with the Capitals. He was named Rookie of the Year in 2006 and has continued to stand out since. Though "The Great 8" has enjoyed his entire NHL career playing with the Caps, in 2014, Ovechkin returned to his native country to play on the Russian Olympic team.

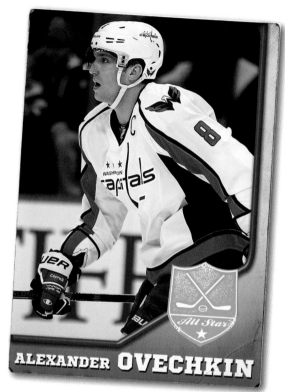

ALEXANDER OVECHKIN

"You dive into sport with your head and arms and legs, and there's no time for anything else. "
– Alex Ovechkin

STATS

Born: 09/17/85
Moscow, Russia

Position: Right Wing
Shoots right

Team: #8 Washington Capitals, Captain

Superstar Centers

- Guy Lafleur helped lead the Montreal Canadiens to five Stanley Cups (1973, 1976–1979) and was the league's top goal scorer for three of those years.

- Jonathan Toews, of the Chicago Blackhawks, is the youngest player to become a member of the "Triple Gold Club"—he has won an Olympic gold medal, a World Championship gold, and the Stanley Cup.

Mario Lemieux

One of the greatest hockey players of all time is Mario Lemieux, who was born in 1965 in Montreal, Quebec. His family loved hockey so much that they had an ice rink on the front lawn, and the future Hall of Famer started learning to play when he was just three years old. In 1984, the Pittsburgh Penguins drafted the young center. On his first shift in the NHL, Lemieux scored a

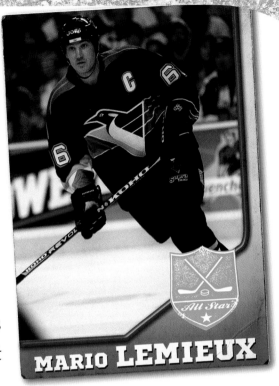

MARIO **LEMIEUX**

goal! Lemieux won two Stanley Cups with the Penguins. He also won Olympic gold as captain of the Canadian team in 2002. He did all this despite battling serious health issues. When he retired as a player, Lemieux bought a share of the Penguins and won another Stanley Cup in 2009, this time as the team's owner.

> "All I can say to the young players is, enjoy every moment of it. Just enjoy every moment of it. Your career goes by very quickly."
> —*Mario Lemieux*

- Russian-born Evgeni Malkin, who centers for the Pittsburgh Penguins, is the first player since 1917 to score goals in each of his first six NHL games.

- Josh Sweeney scored the game winner when the U.S. Paralympic Sled Hockey Team took gold in Sochi. Sweeney, who lost both legs while serving with the U.S. Marines in Afghanistan in 2009, became interested in sled hockey during his rehab. He plays for the San Antonio Rampage.

Patrick Kane

Patrick Kane was the number-one draft pick when the Chicago Blackhawks snatched him up in 2007. That year, the right winger led the team in points and assists and won the Calder Memorial Trophy, awarded to the league's best rookie player. In 2010, Kane had another standout year. He won the silver medal with the U.S. Olympic team. Then, he led the Blackhawks to their first Stanley Cup since 1961 by scoring the winning playoff goal in overtime! This superstar, who is known for rising to the occasion in big games, helped the Blackhawks win a second Stanley Cup in 2013 and took home the title of playoff MVP.

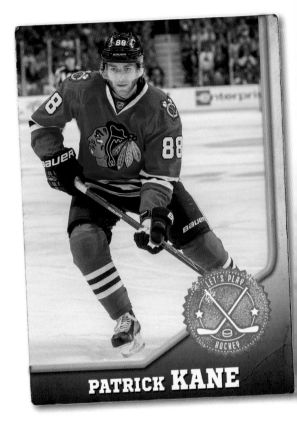

PATRICK **KANE**

Kane chose #88 for the year that he was born.

STATS

Born: 11/19/88
Buffalo, NY, United States

Position: Right Wing
Shoots left

Team: #88 Chicago Blackhawks

Wicked Wingers

- Like father, like son. Brett Hull (right wing) and his dad Bobby Hull (left wing) are the only father-and-son duo in NHL history to each score 1,000 points.

- Left winger Daniel Sedin makes amazing plays for the Vancouver Canucks, often exchanging perfect passes with his identical twin brother Henrik, who plays center.

Jaromir Jagr

This right winger began skating in his native Czechoslovakia when he was three. By 16, he was one of the best hockey players in the country. He was drafted by the Pittsburgh Penguins at 18. It wasn't easy for Jagr to leave his home country. He did not speak English very well and became homesick. But when the team brought another Czech player on board, things picked up and, at 19, he became the youngest player in the NHL to score a goal in the Stanley Cup finals. Jagr won two Stanley Cups with the Penguins. Even as one of 25 hockey players in the Triple Gold Club, Jagr has moved around a lot in the NHL, playing on seven different teams.

Jagr chose #68 for his jersey to honor the year of the Prague Spring Uprising, a political rebellion in his home country.

STATS

Born: 02/15/72
Kladno, Czech Republic

Position: Right Wing
Shoots left

Team: #68 New Jersey Devils

- Cassie Campbell, who played left wing, is the only team captain, male or female, to lead Canada to two gold medals at the Olympics.

- Cammi Granato of the U.S. National Women's Team was the all-time leading scorer in women's international hockey and, in 2012, was inducted into the Hockey Hall of Fame.

DYNAMIC DEFENSE

Defensemen are a goalie's best friends. They sacrifice their bodies to block passes and shots on goal. The best **blueliners** can anticipate what the opposition is going to do—and get in their way. They also move the puck out of their zone. Some defensemen, such as Bobby Orr, are also remembered for scoring goals!

Bobby Orr

This famous defenseman from Parry Sound, Ontario, was a humble team player—who changed the game of hockey forever. Orr had an amazing ability to defend his zone, earning him eight **consecutive** Norris trophies for being the NHL's top defenseman (1968–1976). But, unlike most who went before him, Orr also played offensively. He could score! Orr is the only defenseman who was the top scorer in the entire league (yes, including forwards) twice. In the 1970 Stanley Cup final against the St. Louis Blues, Orr scored the winning goal for the Boston Bruins in overtime.

Orr also scored the winning goal in the 1972 Stanley Cup final.

Zdeno Chara

Slovakian-born Zdeno Chara moved to North America when he was 19. He has played for three NHL teams: the New York Islanders, the Ottawa Senators, and the Boston Bruins. In 2006, he became captain of the Bruins and, three years later, won the Norris trophy for best defenseman. It was well deserved. That year, the Bruins defense allowed the fewest goals into the net of any team in the NHL. In 2011, Chara helped the Bruins win the Stanley Cup with his intense defensive skills. But his talents also go beyond the defensive zone. Chara has the fastest **slap shot** in the NHL—his shots fly at 108.8 miles per hour (175 kph)!

STATS

Born: 03/18/77
Trencin, Slovakia

Position: Defenseman
Shoots left

Team: #33 Boston Bruins, Captain

Cool Fact!

At 6'9" (206 cm) Chara is the tallest player to ever have played in the NHL.

When he was young, Chara was told that his towering height was not a good fit for hockey.

19

Duncan Keith

When he was younger, many people told Duncan Keith that he would never play in the NHL because he was too small. He worked hard to prove them wrong, and he has never stopped. When he was drafted in 2002, he weighed 152 pounds (69 kg). Now, at 200 pounds (91 kg) of muscle, Keith is in amazing shape, which gives him the ability to spend more time on the ice per game than most skaters in the league. The effort has paid off. Keith has won two Norris trophies for top defenseman in the NHL, two Olympic gold medals with Team Canada, and two Stanley Cups.

Keith signed a 13-year deal with the Chicago Blackhawks. He will be with the team until 2022.

STATS

Born: 07/16/83
Winnipeg, MB, Canada

Position: Defenseman
Shoots left

Team: #2 Chicago Blackhawks

Daring Defense

- In 2014, L.A. Kings defenseman Drew Doughty became the eighth player ever to win the Olympic hockey gold and Stanley Cup in the same year.

- Andy Yohe played roller hockey with an Iowa team as a teen. After losing his legs in an accident, he found a new way to play and a career. Yohe won gold with the U.S. Paralympic Sled Hockey Team in Vancouver in 2010 and Sochi in 2014. He also helps other amputees with their prosthetic limbs.

Shea Weber

This 6′4″, 233-pound (193 cm and 106 kg) blueliner isn't afraid to throw his weight around. For the opposition's offense, trying to get past Weber is like trying to break through a wall—a wall that's jumping out and checking them! The Nashville Predators' captain is as comfortable in the attack zone as he is in the defensive zone. Like Bobby Orr, Weber has a great all-around game and plays offensively. In the Vancouver Olympics, while playing for his native Canada, Weber's slap shot ripped through the net, straight through to the boards.

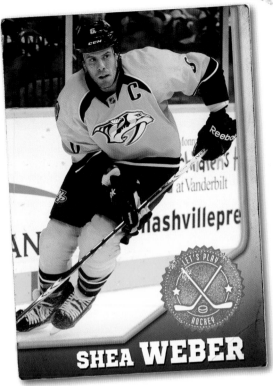

Weber shoots so hard that he has been known to shatter glass.

> "As a kid you always dream of getting a goal in the NHL....It's good to be here now and see what it's like."
>
> – Shea Weber

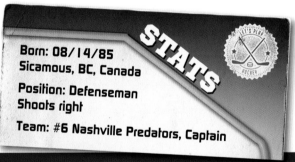

STATS

Born: 08/14/85
Sicamous, BC, Canada

Position: Defenseman
Shoots right

Team: #6 Nashville Predators, Captain

- Montreal Canadiens star defenseman P. K. Subban chose the position when his father told him that many people could play forward and score, but not many could play back and still score the way P.K. did. Subban won the Norris trophy in 2013.

- Geraldine Heaney has been compared to the legendary Bobby Orr for her ability to play defense. She was inducted into the Hockey Hall of Fame in 2013.

Some people say that a team is only as good as its goalie. The best goalies are flexible and have killer reflexes. They can anticipate where the puck is going to go, based on its speed and angle, and swiftly block shots with their body, glove, or stick.

Patrick Roy

As one of the best goaltenders in the history of the NHL, Patrick Roy (nicknamed "Saint Patrick") played calmly under pressure. This led him to three playoff MVP titles and four Stanley Cups—two with the Montreal Canadiens and two with the Colorado Avalanche. Both teams have retired his number. Roy led the league in shutouts twice in his career and, at the time he retired in 2003, he had won more games than any other goaltender in the NHL (551). Roy is still a force in hockey as head coach of the Colorado Avalanche. He was named the NHL's best coach in 2014.

PATRICK ROY

Roy won three Vezina trophies for being the NHL's best goaltender.

Martin Brodeur

Martin Brodeur is an expert at maneuvering on his skates, getting in position, and chasing down loose pucks. He has many types of saves in his bag of tricks—in addition to being able to **butterfly** with the best of them, he plays well on his feet and has an awesome glove hand. Since the three **shutouts** in his first season with the New Jersey Devils, when he was Rookie of the Year, his trophy case has filled up with three Stanley Cups, an Olympic gold medal, four best goaltender trophies, and many more. Brodeur is also remembered for scoring the winning goal on the Canadiens' empty net during the 1997 playoffs.

STATS

Born: 05/06/72
Montreal, QC, Canada

Position: Goaltender
Catches left

Team: #30 New Jersey Devils

Cool Fact!

Brodeur and his father Denis, who was also a goalie, are the only father-and-son goalkeepers to both win medals at the Olympics. Denis won bronze for Canada in 1956.

Brodeur has beaten Roy's record for most wins in regular season play. He is now at 688 (and 124 shutouts).

Carey Price

When Carey Price was growing up, the closest indoor rink was a 200-mile (322 km) drive from his hometown in British Columbia. His dad, a former goalie, taught him to play when the creek froze in the winters. When Price was nine, they decided he needed to play organized hockey. His dad drove for hours—or flew their four-seater plane—to take Carey to practices. It was all worth it. After a rocky start with the Montreal Canadiens in 2008, Price quickly became their number-one goaltender and now ranks in the top 10 in most NHL goalkeeping stats.

Price helped the Canadian team win the gold medal at the 2014 Olympics.

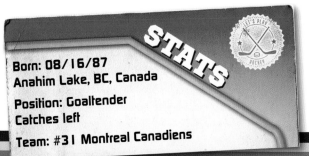

STATS

Born: 08/16/87
Anahim Lake, BC, Canada

Position: Goaltender
Catches left

Team: #31 Montreal Canadiens

Great Goalies

- Tuukka Rask is a force in the net for the Boston Bruins and won the trophy for best goaltender in the NHL in 2014. He also led his home country Finland to a bronze medal with a shutout game against the U.S. in the 2014 Olympics.

- In 2010, when Shannon Szabados was goalie for the Canadian women's team in the Olympics, she got a shutout in the gold medal win against the U.S. and was named the Olympics' top goaltender.

Jonathan Quick

This star goalie began playing with the L.A. Kings in the 2007–08 season. Jonathan Quick has a fitting last name—he moves to the puck like lightning. He won his first Stanley Cup with the Kings in 2012 and was also a major factor in their most recent Cup victory in 2014. He made 32 saves to shut out the New York Rangers in Game 3.

Quick was MVP of the 2012 Stanley Cup playoffs.

STATS

Born: 01/21/86
Milford, CT, United States

Position: Goaltender
Catches left

Team: #32 Los Angeles Kings

"How would you like a job where, every time you make a mistake, a big red light goes on and 18,000 people boo?"
– *Jacques Plante*

- In 1959, Jacques Plante literally changed the face of hockey when he became the first goalie to wear a mask. After a slap shot that resulted in 200 stitches to his face, he refused to get back on the ice without one.

- Goalie Corbin Watson led Canada to the 2013 IPC World Sledge Hockey Championships, then to a bronze medal at Sochi in 2014. He lost a leg in a car accident in 2006 when he was a teen. He is known for shutting out his opponents.

STARS OFF THE ICE

While hockey's superstar players grab the attention of the fans, some of the most important "players" in the game stand off to the side.

Scotty Bowman: The Coach

Arguably the best hockey coach of all time, Scotty Bowman has led three different teams to the Stanley Cup and has had his name engraved on the trophy nine times. Bowman originally wanted to play pro hockey but, when he suffered a concussion while playing in the juniors, he changed his plans. Luckily for his players, Bowman decided to become a coach. The NHL's all-time coaching leader was a genius when it came to strategy. He could read other teams and determine what it would take to win, then motivate his players to do exactly that.

Scotty Bowman (right) was inducted into the Hockey Hall of Fame in 1991.

Cool Fact!

Scotty Bowman's son Stan, who is now the Blackhawks' vice president and general manager, was named after the Stanley Cup.

Joel Quenneville: Coach Q

Part of being a great coach is being able to motivate players and bring out the best in them. Joel Quenneville (aka Coach Q) is often called a "player's coach." He understands what each member of the team needs because he spent 13 years playing in the NHL himself. His approachable style and his ability to communicate with the players was a factor in his Stanley Cup wins: first as assistant coach with the Colorado Avalanche (1996) and later with the Chicago Blackhawks (2010, 2013).

Coach Q won the Jack Adams award for Coach of the Year in 2000 when he was with the St. Louis Blues.

Fraser studied at Haliburton Referee School and NHL training camp for officials.

Kerry Fraser: The Ref

The officials in the striped shirts may have the toughest job in hockey—enforcing the rules. They must also deal with players, fans, and coaches questioning their every call (not always nicely). Kerry Fraser saw it all in the record-setting 2,165 games he officiated. Whether they agreed with all of his calls, fans and players respected him. As a former hockey player himself, Fraser understood the game and was fair. He was also fast on his skates—able to get in position to see the plays, but also get out of the way quickly!

FUTURE SUPERSTARS

Luckily for fans of the game, the story of hockey has no ending. It is still being written as superstars-in-the-making get on the ice and train so that someday they may be as good as—or even better than—their own hockey heroes.

Nathan MacKinnon

Growing up, Nathan MacKinnon plastered his walls with posters of his favorite player Sidney Crosby. Soon, MacKinnon's own picture might be inspiring other young players. He was selected first overall in the 2013 NHL draft by the Colorado Avalanche and, at 18, is the youngest person to play with the team. The center/winger dominated in his first year, intimidating the opposition with his high level of play. He was Rookie of the Year in 2014.

MacKinnon's teammates call him "The Kid."

STATS

Born: 09/01/95
Halifax, NS, Canada

Position: Center
Shoots right

Team: #29 Colorado Avalanche

Seth Jones

In 2013, Seth Jones was drafted by the Nashville Predators to play defense. He stood out in the junior leagues and was a member of the 2013 World Junior Ice Hockey Championships gold-medal winning team.

STATS

Born: 10/03/94
Arlington, TX, United States

Position: Defenseman
Shoots right

Team: #3 Nashville Predators

Jones is the son of Popeye Jones, who played and now coaches pro basketball.

Marie-Philip Poulin

This two-time Olympian made her mark on hockey with unbelievable goals that led the Canadian team to gold medals in the 2010 and 2014 Olympics. In 2010, Poulin scored both goals in the 2-0 gold-medal game against the United States. In 2014, Canada was trailing 2-1 against the U.S. With 55 seconds to go in the third period, Poulin swept in and scored. Then, she got the "**Golden Goal**" in overtime, putting Canada on top of the podium!

MARIE-PHILIP **POULIN**

Poulin also plays for Boston University.

BECOMING A HOCKEY SUPERSTAR

Do you dream of following in the footsteps of your hockey heroes? Becoming a superstar player takes passion and commitment. All of the people in this book have worked extremely hard to reach such a high level of play. They have spent countless hours on the ice doing drills and practicing their positions. Off the ice, they eat healthy and stay fit. They have dedicated their lives to the sport that they love.

Hockey for Fun

Only a small percentage of players end up in the NHL. The best reason to play hockey is for the pure fun of it. What could be better than lacing up your skates, grabbing your stick, and heading out to play with your friends? No matter where the sport takes you, if you are enjoying the game while you are on the ice, you win!

LEARNING MORE

Can't get enough of hockey's amazing superstars? Check out these books and websites for more information.

Books

Hockey Legends in the Making by Shane Frederick, Sports Illustrated Kids, 2014

The Ultimate Collection of Pro Hockey Records by Shane Frederick, Sports Illustrated Kids, 2015

Hockey Superstars 2014–2015 by Paul Romanuk, Scholastic Canada, 2014

Websites

NHL: National Hockey League
This site features NHL standings and schedules, as well as information on teams and players. Click on links to the players' sites to learn all about your favorites.
www.nhl.com

Hockey Hall of Fame
The best players of all time are celebrated in the Hockey Hall of Fame. Visit this website to view photos or read the Stanley Cup Journal and Legends Spotlight.
www.hhof.com

GLOSSARY

Note: Some boldfaced words are defined where they appear in the book.

amateur When someone plays for fun without pay

blueliners Defensemen

butterfly A style of goaltending where the goalie drops down to cover the lower half of the net with their leg pads

consecutive Following one after the other in a series

dekes Fakes an opponent out of position

draft A selection process in which teams pick players for their teams

Golden Goal The gold-medal winning goal at the Olympics

memorabilia (sports) A collection of sports-related objects or materials

opposition The team being played against

rookie A first-year player in a professional sport

scouts People who evaluate talent

shutouts Games in which one team prevents the opposing team from scoring

slap shot Hitting the puck with the blade of the stick after taking a full backswing

INDEX